The 45-Second Presentation That *Will* Change Your Life

The World's Best-Selling Network Marketing Guide

Don Failla

ROOFTOP
publishing

RoofTop Publishing™
1663 Liberty Drive, Suite 200
Bloomington, IN 47403
Phone: 1-800-839-8640

First published by AuthorHouse 6/28/2006

ISBN: 1-60008-009-X (sc)

Library of Congress Control Number 2006928569

Printed in the United States of America
Bloomington, Indiana

This book is printed on acid-free paper.

"Withhold not good from them to whom it is due,
when it is in the power of thine hand to do it."
—Proverbs 3:27, KJV

Dedication

This book is dedicated to the free enterprise system, which we all have the opportunity to enjoy, and without which network markcting would be impossible.

Contents

Preface

The 45-Second Presentation

Have you ever thought about what it would be like to own your life? This is what I think it means to "own your life": When you subtract out the sleeping time, commuting time, working time, and things you have to do each and every day of your life, most people don't have more than one to two hours a day to do what they would like to do—and then, if they did, would they have the money to do it?

We have discovered a way people can learn how to "own their lives" by building a home-based business; and we have a system for doing it that is so simple anyone can do it. It doesn't require selling, and the best part is, it won't take much of your time.

The 45-Second Presentation is all one needs to know to start building a large organization. In fact, if one cannot learn this presentation, he can read it to a friend or put it on a 3 x 5 card and let friends read it for themselves.

Beyond this presentation, you do not need to know anything. Once you realize and understand this, you can introduce your business to anyone, because absolutely anyone can build a business if he wants to. All you really need is a little desire. Without desire, you have nothing.

The secret to the system we teach is not to talk. Talking is your worst enemy. The more you talk, the more the prospects think they cannot do what you are doing. The more you talk, the more they think they don't have time. Remember, time is the number one excuse people have for not getting started.

After your friends read the 45-Second Presentation, they may ask you a question. Regardless of what the question is, if you answer it, you lose. They will have five more questions before you know it. You will be bouncing all over the place! Simply tell them that they will have a lot of questions and that the system is designed to answer most of them. Have them read the first four Napkin Presentations and then get back to you.

Never tell prospects to read the book. They will set it on the shelf and get to it in due time. Tell them to read the first four Napkin Presentations. They will read them right away, and over 90 percent will finish the book at the same time.

After reading the book, your prospects will understand network marketing. This is important because the number one reason people don't do the business is because they don't understand it. Once they understand network marketing, they are ready for you to present your vehicle, company, products, and marketing plan. But I said you don't have to know anything other than the 45-Second Presentation to get started. So now what do you do?

At this point, you would use the tools or your team to do the talking for you. Tools would be brochures, audiotapes, and videotapes from your company. Your team would be your immediate up-line starting with the person who is your sponsor.

Let's say you have your first prospect! You have done the 45-Second Presentation, and he has read the book. You invite your prospect to meet you for lunch. Let him know that you will also be inviting your sponsor, who can explain the business on your behalf.

(Key point: Who pays for lunch? You do. Your sponsor is working for you. How many times would you have to buy your sponsor lunch or dinner before you could explain the business on your own?)

A man came up to us at a seminar in Germany and said, "Not only do you not need to know anything to get started, you could also have a *free lunch every day* when you are working for your down-line."

Happy eating and watch your business grow!

Chapter 1

Introduction to Network Marketing

The purpose of this book is to convey to you the reader, through illustrations and examples, just what network marketing is and what it is not. We will also show you how you can effectively—I repeat, effectively—explain network marketing to others.

This book should be treated as a training manual. It is intended to be used as a tool to help you train the people in your organization. Include it in their initial "kit" of information about your program.

I have developed the "Napkin Presentations" upon which this book is based over the last several years, since about 1973. I have been involved in network marketing to one degree or another since 1969. This book will cover the ten presentations developed thus far.

Before going into the details of the ten Napkin Presentations, allow me to answer one of the most frequently asked and probably the most basic of all the questions: "What is network marketing?"

First, you must understand that network marketing is the modern term used for multi-level marketing (MLM). So, in order to understand network marketing, you must understand multi-level marketing. Let's break it down. *Marketing* simply means "moving a product or service from the manufacturer or provider to the consumer." *Multi-level* refers to the system of compensation provided to those persons who are causing the product to move or the service to be provided. *Multi* means "more than one." *Level* refers to what may better be termed as "generation." It could be called "multi-generation marketing." We shall stay with "multi-level" since that is what is most common. It is so common, in fact, that many illegal pyramids and chain distribution schemes or chain letters have tried to pass themselves off as being a multi-level program. This has created such a stigma, although unjustified, that many of the newer multi-level marketing companies are using other names for their type of marketing. Some of the names you will hear are "uni-level marketing," "co-op mass marketing," and the more popular "network marketing."

There are really only three basic methods of moving products. (Hold up three fingers as you demonstrate this point.)

1) RETAILING—I'm sure everyone is familiar with retailing. The grocery store, the drug store, the department store ... you go into a store and buy something.

2) DIRECT SALES—This would usually (but not always) include insurance, cookware, encyclopedias, etc. Fuller Brush, the Avon lady, Tupperware home parties, etc. are some examples of direct sales efforts.

3) NETWORK MARKETING—This is the one we shall be discussing in this book. It should not be confused with the other two, especially with the direct sales method, with which network marketing commonly is confused.

A fourth type of marketing that is sometimes added to the list (hold up the fourth finger) is mail order. Mail order can be a network marketing type but most generally is included in the direct sales category.

A fifth type, often confused with network marketing, is pyramid sales. (Hold out your thumb for illustration.) The fact is, pyramids are illegal! One of the main reasons they are illegal is their failure to move a product or to provide a valid service. If a product doesn't move, how can you even call it "marketing," let alone "network marketing"? Pyramids may include networking—but MARKETING THEY ARE NOT!

Most objections that people have about getting into network marketing are due to their not realizing the differences between network marketing and the direct sales method of marketing. This confusion is understandable because most reputable network marketing companies belong to the Direct Selling Association.

You have been conditioned, perhaps, to think of them as door-to-door direct sales programs because your first encounter with them was when a distributor knocked on your door to sell you something.

However, there are some features that differentiate network marketing from retail and direct sales companies. One very significant difference is that in network marketing you are in business for yourself but not by yourself.

By being in business for yourself, whether or not but especially if you are operating out of your home, you may be entitled to some substantial tax breaks. We won't get into tax advantages in this book. Most people can get that information from their accountant or from the many books that have been written on the subject. However, you should be aware of this benefit.

Being in business for yourself, you are buying the products wholesale from the company you are representing. This means that you can (and should) use these items for your own consumption. Many people get involved in a company at first for this reason alone, to buy wholesale. And many of those will get "serious."

Since you are buying your products wholesale, you can, if you wish to, sell those products at retail and make a profit. The most common misunderstanding about network marketing is the notion that you *have to* sell retail to be successful. There is a lot to be said for selling retail and it should not be ignored. Some programs even require that a retail quota be met in order to qualify for a bonus. You may sell if you want to or have to due to your particular program's requirements, but in regard to making the larger sums of income, the real success is in building the organization.

Important point: Let your sales come as the natural result of building the organization. More people fail than succeed by trying to do it the other way around—they try to build the organization by emphasizing selling. As you read through the Napkin Presentations that follow, you will see this concept unfold before you.

The word "selling" triggers negative thoughts in the minds of about 95 percent of the people. In network marketing, you don't need to "sell" the products in the traditional sense of the word. However, product does have to move or nobody gets paid. I define selling as "calling on strangers trying to sell them something they may neither need nor want." Again, PRODUCT HAS TO MOVE OR NOBODY GETS PAID!

When you build an organization, you are actually building a network through which to channel your products. Retailing is the foundation of network marketing. Sales in network marketing come from distributors sharing with their friends, neighbors, and relatives. They never have to talk to strangers.

To build a large successful business, you need a BALANCE. You need to sponsor and teach network marketing, and in the process of doing this, you can build a customer base by retailing to your friends, neighbors, and relatives.

Don't try to sell the world on your program yourself. Remember that network marketing is building an organization in which a lot of distributors all retail a little. This is far better than a few trying to do it all.

With virtually all the network marketing companies, the need to spend large sums of money on advertising is non-existent. Advertising is done almost exclusively by word of mouth. For this reason, they have more money to put into product development. As a result, they usually have a higher quality product than their counterpart found in retail stores. You can share with friends a high-quality product of a type that they are already using. You're simply replacing their old brand with something that you have discovered through your own experience to be better.

So you see, it's not going door to door every day calling on strangers. All network marketing programs that I know of teach that if you simply SHARE the quality of their products or services with friends, that is all the "selling" that is involved. (We prefer to call it "sharing," because that's what it is!)

Another thing that differentiates network marketing from direct sales is the SPONSORING of other distributors. In direct sales and even in some network marketing companies, it's called "recruiting."

However, "sponsoring" and "recruiting" are definitely not the same thing. You sponsor someone then teach him how to do what you are doing—building a business of his own.

We emphasize that there is a big difference between sponsoring someone and just "signing him up." When you sponsor someone, you are making a COMMITMENT to him. If you are not willing to make that commitment, then you are doing him a disservice by signing him up.

At this point, all you need to be is willing to help someone build a business of his own. This book will be an invaluable tool in showing you how to do just that.

It is a responsibility of sponsors to teach the people they bring into a business all they know about that business—things such as ordering products, keeping records, how to get started, how to build and train their organization, etc. This book will go a long way toward making you able to meet that responsibility.

Sponsoring is what makes a network marketing business grow. As your organization grows, you are building toward becoming an independent, successful businessperson. You are your own boss!

With direct selling companies, you work for the company. If you decide to quit that company and move to another area, you end up having to start all over again. In almost all of the network marketing programs that I am aware of, you can move to another area of the country and sponsor people without losing the volume generated by the group you left behind.

In network marketing programs, you can make a lot of money. It takes a little longer with some companies than it does with others, but making a lot of money comes from building an organization, not by just selling the product. To be sure, you can make a good living in some programs by just selling the product—but you can make a *fortune* by building an organization as your primary function.

People will get started in a network marketing business with the idea of making $50, $100, or even $200 per month, and suddenly they will realize that if they want to get serious about the business, they could be making $1,000 or $2,000 per month—or more. Again, remember that a person doesn't make that kind of money by just selling the products… he makes that kind of money by building an organization.

That is the purpose of this book: to teach you the things you need to know to be able to build an organization quickly and to develop certain and proper attitudes about network marketing. If a person thinks network marketing is illegal, having the same connotation of a pyramid (and some do make that assumption), you are going to have trouble sponsoring him.

You must teach your prospects the facts to eliminate their mistaking a true network marketing organization as being a pyramid. One example you could show them is the illustration at the right. The pyramid is built from the top down, and only those in at the very beginning can ever be near the top.

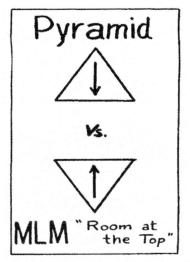

In the network marketing—or multi-level marketing (MLM)—triangle, everybody starts at the bottom and has the opportunity to build a large organization.

One can build an organization many times larger than his sponsor's organization if he wants.

The main objective is to get your prospect into a general discussion concerning network marketing and explain, with your three fingers, the differences between retailing, direct sales, and network marketing. Then you may have a good start at sponsoring him into your particular network marketing vehicle.

Most people don't realize that network marketing is big business! Network marketing has been in our midst for about thirty-five years now. Some companies that have been around for twenty years or so are already doing a billion dollars per year by themselves.

We know of one company that did over $2 million in its first year of operation. In its second year, it went over $15 million. For its third year, it projected $75 million. Its goal is to reach ONE BILLION per year by the end of its fifth year. The principles expounded in this book will make that goal reachable. That's a pretty fast start in anybody's league!

Network marketing is one of the viable ways for an inventor or manufacturer to put a new product on the market without having a million dollars and without having to totally give up his product to someone else.

Notes

Notes

Chapter II

Napkin Presentation #1
"Two Times Two Is Four"

You can show a person this one *before* he sees the program or the vehicle you want to share. It is an absolute must to show your prospect this presentation as soon as possible after you have introduced him to your program. You want his thinking to be going in the right direction from day one. What this will do is take the proverbial "monkey off his back" in thinking he has to go out and "sponsor the world" to make a large amount of money in network marketing.

This presentation will also show the prospect how important it is to work with his people and help them to get started.

This presentation starts by writing down "2 x 2 = 4," and multiplying on down as shown in the figure at the right.

We tell a joke that if you sponsor someone who can't do this right here, pass, because you are going to have trouble working with him.

$$
\begin{array}{r}
2 \\
\times 2 \\
\hline
4 \\
\times 2 \\
\hline
8 \\
\times 2 \\
\hline
16
\end{array}
$$

Notice that we start using the word "sponsor" now. To the right of the 2 x 2 column, write 3 x 3, saying, "Over here you sponsor three people, and you teach [We also start to use the word "teach"] these three to sponsor three, making nine more. Then you teach your three people how to teach those nine to sponsor, and now you have twenty-seven. Going on down one more level, you will have eighty-one." Notice the difference between sixteen and eighty-one. Bring it to his attention and ask him if he would agree that it's a pretty good difference. Then point out to him that the real difference is ONE! Everybody only sponsored one more! You will usually pick up some reaction from this, but continue right on; it gets better.

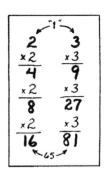

Let's say you sponsor four people into the business. Moving to the right of the 3 x 3 column, you again run down a column of figures, writing them down as you speak.

"Let's see what happens if everybody sponsored only two more." As you continue to write, you say, "You sponsor four and teach them to sponsor four. Then you help your four to teach the sixteen they have to sponsor four, adding sixty-four to your group. Work down only one more level, and before you know it, your group has 256 more."

And again you point out, "Now that's getting to be a considerable difference right there, but the…"

You will usually catch some sort of reaction again as he begins to pick up on the concept, and cutting in, he will say before you do, "The real difference is that everybody only sponsored two more!"

We end it with five. The prospect will usually pick up on it by now and mentally or verbally follow right along with you as you write in the final column of figures. By now you can leave out "sponsoring" and "teaching," writing down the figures and commenting, "Five times five is twenty-five, times five is 125, times five is 625. Now that is a fantastic difference!" Again now, the real difference is that everybody only had to sponsor three more.

Most people can relate to sponsoring one, two, or three more, but usually find it difficult to relate to the figures on the bottom line (sixteen, eighty-one, 256, and 625).

So picture yourself in the last column, having had the time to sponsor five serious people into the program. The "5" at the top of the column represents the ones you sponsored who want to get serious about building a business of their own. You may have to sponsor ten, fifteen, or twenty people to get these five.

However, once you totally understand all ten of the Napkin Presentations, you will find that your people will get serious quicker than the people who come into organizations and don't know this material. This book will teach you how to work with them so they will get serious quicker.

Notice in the figure at the right that when you have sponsored five, and they have sponsored five, and so forth, right on down the line, you add all these (circled figures) up and you will have 780 serious people in your organization. Doing this will help you answer the question "Doesn't somebody have to sell the product?" You've all heard that question before if you've been at all active. So just go through this Napkin Presentation with them and explain that two times two is four... right on up to 780 distributors.

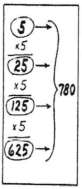

In any kind of network marketing organization, if you have 780 people just USING the product themselves, you have a tremendous volume. (And we haven't even included those who are not serious but are just "product buyers.")

Now, if they all have two, three, four, or five friends ... let's just say they all had ten customers from among their friends, relatives, and acquaintances, that's 7,800 customers! Add to that the 780 distributors in your organization—do you think 8,580 customers plus the "product buyers" will be able to provide you with a profitable enterprise? That's how you make a lot of money in any business—by having a lot of people doing a little bit. But remember, you are only working with five serious people, not a whole army!

We run into people constantly in other network marketing programs, as well as our own, who are amazed at how fast our own organizations have grown. They have been in their programs longer than we have but are scratching the "think tank" on top of their necks and asking, "What are you doing that I'm not doing?"

Our response to them is, "How many people in your front line are you working with?" (The front line are those people directly sponsored by you. They are also called your "first-level" distributors.)

I will usually hear figures anywhere from twenty-five to fifty or more. I know people in network marketing who have over one hundred in their front line, and I'll guarantee you that once you understand the principles outlined in this book, you'll pass those people up in six months, even though they have been in their organizations for six to eight years.

As we go into Napkin Presentation #2, covering the "Salesman Failure Syndrome" in network marketing, I will give you a simple parallel showing why having so many front line people isn't good.

Consider the army, the navy, the air force, the marines, or the coast guard. From the lowest private up to the top brass in the Pentagon, nobody has more than five or six people they are trying to directly supervise. (There may be rare exceptions.) Think about it! Here we have West Point and Annapolis with over two hundred years of experience each, and they don't think anybody should supervise more than five or six people. So you tell me why people get into a network marketing organization and think they can effectively work with fifty people in their front line. They can't do it! That's why a lot of them fail, and you'll see why as you read on.

You shouldn't try to work with more than five serious people at a time. However, make sure that when you sponsor them, you start working down-group. There is a point when they won't need you and then can break away and start another line on their own. This will free you up to work with yet another serious person, keeping your number of those that you are working closely with at five. Some programs may allow you to be effective with only three or four at a time, but none that I know of can be effectively built with more than five.

These Napkin Presentations fairly well tie together, and therefore, some of the questions you may have at this point will be cleared up as you read on.

Chapter III

Napkin Presentation #2
"Salesman Failure Syndrome"

Why do so many salesmen fail when working in a network marketing business? This second presentation will clarify the common mistakes made by sales-oriented professionals.

We shall present to you why we would rather sponsor ten teachers than ten salesmen.

Now, don't get me wrong; I think professional salesmen can be a tremendous asset to your organization—if, like everyone else, they go through the ten Napkin Presentations and thoroughly understand them.

Most people get confused by the statement above, but remember, they still don't understand that network marketing is a method of marketing. We ARE NOT sponsoring people into a direct sales organization. We ARE sponsoring them into a network marketing program.

Much of the time, the problem you will have with a salesman is that when he sees the high quality of the products you represent, he just launches out and takes off, so to speak. Salesmen can put their own presentations together—they don't need us to tell them how to sell; they're the professionals. The point is, we don't want to tell them how to sell. We just want to teach them how to teach and sponsor and build a large, successful network marketing organization. And they, and anyone for that matter, can do just that without selling anything in the normal sense and definition of the word "selling."

If you can't sit down with them and explain a few simple things about network marketing, and how it is different from direct selling, then the tendency is for them to go off in the wrong direction. As we continue on with the Napkin Presentations, we will give you a few examples.

Most people (and especially salesmen) think that if you sponsor someone, you have duplicated your effort. (Draw one circle under the other.) There was one, and now there are two. It sounds logical, but it's not true.

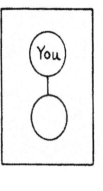

The reason that it's not true is that if the one represented by the top circle (sponsor) goes away, the one he sponsored will go away also; he won't continue on. You must explain to your people that if they truly want to duplicate themselves, they have to be at least three levels deep; only then are they duplicated.

If your sponsor dropped out before you had an opportunity to see that the program really will work, you most likely will assume that it doesn't because it didn't for him. After all, he's your sponsor and certainly must know more about it than you. Let's say that you're here. (Draw a circle and put "You" in the middle of it.) You sponsor Tom. (Draw another circle under the one with "You" in it, write "Tom" in it, and connect the circles with a line.) Now, if you leave and Tom doesn't know what to do (because you haven't taught him), then that's the end of it. But if you do teach Tom how to sponsor, and he sponsors Carol, you are only beginning to duplicate yourself.

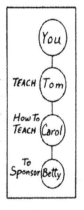

But if Tom doesn't learn how to teach Carol to sponsor, then again it will fizzle out and that's the end of it. You have to teach Tom how to teach Carol how to sponsor. Then she can sponsor Betty or whomever.

Now you are three deep. If you go away (to work with someone else or to a different area of the country), this sub-group will continue on. I emphasize: YOU HAVE TO GO THREE DEEP! You have nothing until you are three deep, and only then are you duplicated.

If you never communicate anything but this one point to the people you sponsor, then you will have the key that will make you more successful than most others in network marketing programs.

Here's what happens to the "salesman": He looks at the demonstrations of the products and hears or reads the testimonials of the results others have had with their use and how they work. Armed with this information, just get out of his way, and he will go out and "sell like crazy"—remember, he's a SALESMAN! He has been in the direct selling business and doesn't have any problem calling on strangers.

Great! So you say to your super-salesman (let's call him Charlie), "Charlie, if you want to make the big bucks, you cannot do it by yourself. You need to sponsor people."

So what does Charlie do? He goes out and sponsors, sponsors, sponsors... He will just sponsor up a storm. A good "salesman" in a network marketing program could sponsor three or four people per week.

But here is what happens: It gets to a point (and it doesn't take long) that people are dropping out as fast as they are being added. If you don't work with them effectively (and you can't be effective if you are trying to work with more than five at a time), you will see them becoming discouraged and giving up.

So Charlie, being discouraged and a little bit impatient, doesn't think anything is happening and he goes off to look for something else to sell. The person who sponsored Charlie, thinking Charlie was going to make him rich, gets discouraged and gives up also.

Most people who have made it big in network marketing don't have a sales background. They may not be teachers professionally, but most of them come from a background with an element of teaching in it. I know of one teacher and school principal who, after only twenty-four months in a network marketing program, was earning in excess of FIFTEEN THOUSAND DOLLARS PER MONTH. He did it and is doing it by teaching others how to do it also.

Let's put some numbers in Charlie's approach so we can more clearly see where he went wrong. We will assume that Charlie, being the super-salesman that he is, went out and sponsored 130 people. Let's also say that he got each of them to sponsor five others, adding 650 more for a total of 780 in his organization. (Sound familiar?)

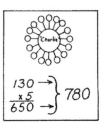

Ask your people this question when you show this to them: "Which do you feel you could do more quickly, sponsor five people who are serious and teach them how to teach, or...?"

Incidentally, the question will come up, "What do I teach them?" The answer is: You teach them what you are learning right here in this book—the ten Napkin Presentations. They need to have an understanding of all ten, but initially the first four.

Teach them that 2 x 2 = 4, and why people fail, etc.

How long do you think it would take you to sponsor 130 people? How many of the first ones would be left when you sponsored number 130? You would find that you are losing them pretty fast. Yet you will discover the retention rate on the 780 in Napkin Presentation #1 to be quite high.

Once you show this to a salesman and he understands it, he will say, "Aha! Now I see what I've got to do..." and he will go do it.

Caution: You must hold salesmen back. Because they don't understand what we have just gone over in this chapter, most people in network marketing will literally encourage their people right out of the business! They will sponsor someone and their new distributor will come to them and say, "Hey, I got five new people last week!" So they say, "Great!" and encouragingly slap him on the back. The following week he signs up five more people. What has become of the five he signed up the first week? They're gone.

If you understand this "Salesman Failure Syndrome," you can still encourage your salesmen, but at the same time stress the point of how important it is to take those first five they sponsored and help them get started.

After I have sponsored someone, it's more important for me to go with him and help him sponsor someone else than it is for me to go out and sponsor another person for myself. I just cannot emphasize this point too much. This point will come up again in a couple of other presentations.

Of the ten Napkin Presentations, the first four are really a must. If you don't have time for all of them, at least get started with #1 and #2 (chapters two and three). You can show them to someone, depending on how much you elaborate, in as quickly as five to ten minutes, once you have practiced them.

In one of the programs I was involved in, I sponsored this fellow named Carl. Carl told me about his sponsoring his daughter in Tennessee and that she knew everybody in town. I was talking to Carl on the phone and related to him that I thought it was great. I quickly added, however, that I needed to tell him something to pass on to his daughter. I asked him if he had a piece of paper and pencil handy (which he did), and I had him write down 2 x 2 = 4 and right on through it. I instructed him to immediately phone his daughter and let her know the mistakes to avoid to get her started in the right direction. He did call her, and it's working out very well for both of them.

Notes

Notes

Chapter IV

Napkin Presentation #3
"Four Things You Have To Do"

In the first presentation, we told you some of the things to do, and in the second presentation, we told you some things not to do, as far as working in depth with your organization. In this Napkin Presentation, we will show you four things you HAVE TO DO to be successful in a network marketing program. These four things are an absolute must! Everybody in network marketing who is making $100,000 or $200,000 per year (and more) did and are doing these four things.

To help you remember these four things, we have paralleled the points to a story that you can relate to your people. They will not only pick up on the parallel but will remember the "have to do's" also.

The story goes like this: Let's imagine you want to take a trip in the family car and leave rainy Washington (it really isn't as bad as some people like to make it out to be) and drive to sunny California. The sunshine in California will represent reaching the top in the program that you're in. When you get there, you are successful—you're at the top!

The first thing that you have to do is GET IN and GET STARTED. There isn't anybody in network marketing who has made a lot of money without first getting started. The amount of money it takes to get started depends on the company and the program you choose as your "vehicle." It can range from nothing on up to $12.50, $45, $100, $200, or even $500 or more.

The second thing you need to do as you take this trip is buy gas and oil. As you travel to California (the top), you will use up the fuel and oil (products), and it will be necessary to replace them. Network marketing works best with products that are consumable. You will use the products up and buy them again, and again, and… What this equates to is you must USE THE PRODUCTS of the company you represent.

Remember, we showed you in Napkin Presentation #1 that with 780 distributors it doesn't matter which program you are in; you will have a very sizable volume.

Naturally, you can see the advantages of building a business with a vehicle that has consumable products. Most network marketing companies are in that category. Non-consumables are usually marketed through retail or direct sales methods, but not always.

The other result of using the products yourself is you will get excited about them. Rather than spend a large sum of money on advertising, network marketing companies put their money into product development and as a result will usually have a higher quality product than that which is normally available in a retail store.

The third thing you have to do is get into HIGH GEAR. Of course you realize that nobody starts out in high gear. We all start out in neutral. (Incidentally, notice that we are not driving an automatic.) We may be in the car, still in the driveway, with the key turned on and the motor racing, but if we never get out of neutral, we will never get to California—or anywhere else for that matter.

To get your car into gear, you must sponsor someone into the business. When you sponsor someone, you are in first gear. We believe you should be in first gear five times, with five serious people. In one of the other presentations, we show you how to determine which of your people are serious.

You will want your five people to get into gear also. You teach them how to get into first gear by sponsoring someone. When each of your five people are in first gear five times, you will be in second gear twenty-five times.

You teach your five people to teach their five to get into first gear five times; they are now in second gear twenty-five times each, and that puts you in third gear 125 times. When you have third-level distributors in your 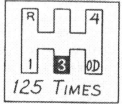 organization, you are in third gear.

Have you noticed how much smoother your car runs in fourth gear? So does your organization! You want to be in high gear (fourth gear) as soon as you can. When your first levels are in third gear, you will be in fourth gear.

Naturally, you want your people to be in high, or fourth, gear as well—and when they are, you are in overdrive.

How do you get into overdrive? You simply help and teach the people you sponsored to get their people into third gear, which puts them into fourth gear and puts you in overdrive.

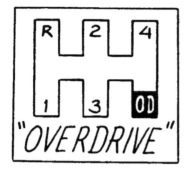

The fourth thing, while you are on your journey to California, is to use the time you have to SHARE your products with the people who are going with you. Let them try them. Let them experience the benefits of the products. When they want to know where they can get them… guess what you do at that point. So share with your friends. For a number of people, this is the retailing part of the business.

At this point, it is important to notice that as we went through Napkin Presentations #1 and #2, and now here is #3, we've told you the four things you have to do to be successful. Not once did we tell you that you have to go out and sell. We don't say that you have to sell the products in the normal sense of the word "sell." We do say that you need to share the products with your friends. You can even share them with strangers. When they see the benefits of your products and your marketing plan, they will become new friends.

You don't even need a large number of customers… say ten, or even less. If all you ever had was ten customers… hey, that's okay. All it means is item number 4 (below) is a very small portion. So what if we cover up the "4" altogether—you could still get to California by doing the first three.

1. GET IN — GET STARTED
2. USE THE PRODUCTS
3. SHIFT INTO HIGH GEAR
4. SHARE WITH FRIENDS (RETAIL)

Notice: If you didn't do number 3 (shift into high gear), and did a lot of number 4, you would never get out of the driveway. (That's what salesmen do.) Once you understand this and tie it in with numbers 1 and 2, you start developing the proper network marketing attitude.

Starting from square one with your new person, you want to get into his subconscious the number five. All you need to do is find five serious people who want to get serious about the business.

When you run into people and ask them how they are doing, you may hear the response, "Gee, I can't find anyone who wants to sell." There's that word "sell" again! Quit looking for people who want to sell! Do start looking for people who want to earn an extra $600, $1,200, or $1,500 per month without having to "go to work" every day. Do you or they know anybody like that? Your answer and theirs, like mine, will be, "Yeah, everybody!" Well, those are the people you want to talk to, because everybody would like to have that kind of dough coming in.

Simply point out that it may take five to ten hours a week of their spare time to build a business. But then we hasten to say, "What's wrong with that?"

People sometimes get into network marketing programs and think somehow it's all going to happen just because they signed up. Not so! Remember, the car we are driving to California does not have an automatic transmission.

I know, and surely you know, people who have gone to college to get a degree, and there is absolutely nothing wrong with that. Maybe you're one of them. You go to school every day. You study all day and half the night, week after week, for years. Then when you finally graduate, how much money can you make?

So give five to ten hours of your time each week to learning the ten Napkin Presentations and everything you can about the network marketing company you are representing. When you learn and understand them, you can teach the Napkin Presentations to others. The book you are now reading is your key to tomorrow's success.

We don't want you to get uptight by thinking you can't teach someone what you are learning here. Sure, this may be the first time you've read or heard these concepts, and we really can't expect you to know it all well enough to teach it. But then you don't have to!

Remember, to get into a network marketing program, you have to have a sponsor. If your sponsor is a real "sponsor," he will help you with your first five people. Notice: It's a helping relationship. In the process of showing the Napkin Presentations to your friends at meetings (one on one or in groups), your sponsor is training you as well.

As a suggestion, we ask that you set some sort of goal for yourself. When you are about 20 percent up the ladder in your program, you should know and understand the ten Napkin Presentations. By the time you get three-quarters of the way, you should be able to teach others. When you are at or near the top, you will be able to teach your people to teach others. It's something beneficial that you can master over a relatively short period of time.

With this book and/or the tape on the same subject, you can sit down and read and study, or listen to the tape again and again and again. If you were given an "assignment" to do the above, and you had to go through the material five, six, or even ten times, and a year from now it meant you could be making two, three, four, or even six thousand dollars a month, is it worth spending five to ten hours a week?

Now, you have to admit, that's a pretty neat way to "go to school," right? Take a look at some of those college textbooks and try to learn what they contain; they're not going to make that kind of money for you!

Welcome to Network Marketing University!

Chapter V

Napkin Presentation #4
"Digging Down to Bedrock"

Discouragement is one of the problems that can beset a new distributor that you have sponsored if you fail to impress upon him the importance of getting a head start. That is why we stress that people do not start counting their months in the business until they have had their training month or their training period of whatever length of time they need.

When they first get into a network marketing organization, they may have a tendency, without a head start, to look up at the leaders way out in front and become discouraged and think they will never be able to catch up.

Draw a picture of a crowd of runners. Note the arrows showing a runner trying to catch up to the crowd and the runner going even faster trying to stay ahead of the others. (You may find it simpler to draw circles to illustrate this point.) Remember when you were in P.E. in school and were running laps? People will run faster to stay ahead of a crowd than to catch up to it. Since there is no "finish line" in this race, you can all be winners. I have a quote from my pastor displayed in my office that reads:

"THE ONLY LOSERS ARE THE QUITTERS."

However, to run a good race, one should train for it. When you sponsor someone, have him consider the first two to six weeks in the business as his training month. The next month will be his starting month.

Everything he reads and listens to, the meetings he attends, getting together with his sponsor and other people, the products he tries, the products he moves—all of this training is giving him a head start on his starting month in the business, which is next month. When next month comes, if he's not yet ready to get serious about the program, consider that he is still in his training month or period. Don't have him start counting his months until he is ready to get serious. That way, when he finally does get serious, he will be "warmed up" for the race and can get off to a head start and run a faster race.

One of the major benefits of all these Napkin Presentations is that as you share them with your new distributors and prospects and have training programs, they have a tendency to become motivators. Every time I show the "2 x 2 = 4" presentation, I get all excited again about the possibilities in network marketing.

Once you read and study and understand what I am going to show you in the following pages, you will be motivated and encouraged every  time you see a new high-rise office building under construction.

Notice that when construction begins it seems like it takes months and months, almost forever, before you see it begin to rise out of the ground. But once it gets above ground level, it seems to rise about one floor per week—it goes up fast!

So picture that tall office building as your own organization as it will be someday, and ponder what you will have to do to get it.

When you first began to sponsor those first five serious people, you were digging the foundation with a shovel or a spade.

But notice that when you dig down into the second level by teaching your people to sponsor—that's twenty-five people now—you have to bring in the bulldozers.

When you have taught your people how to teach the people in their groups to sponsor, you are well on your way to bedrock, and you are now beginning to excavate with steam shovels! When you have begun to see the 125 third-level people, you have reached bedrock.

Now you can start going up. When you are down four deep in your organization, it means you are now starting to "become visible" and your building will rise up quite rapidly.

So, if you have been in the business for several months and don't see anything happening, don't get discouraged; it's just that the foundation is still under construction. It's sort of like the gold prospector who spent months and months digging a mine only to give up and quit when he was just six inches from the main vein.

Again, let's go back to the salesmen. That's what happens to them. They move on to something else just as they were about to hit bedrock and start seeing the building rise. You really can't expect to see visible results of real growth until you have gone down at least four deep. It doesn't necessarily mean you have to be five deep AND four deep; if any one of your lines is four deep, it means you are starting to build floors and are visible.

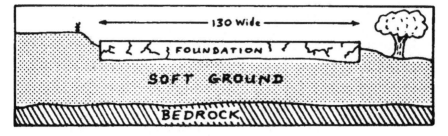

Above is an illustration of what the foundation of the person who sponsors 130 will look like. Notice that he hasn't reached bedrock even if he has sponsored five "product users" or "wholesale buyers" and has a group of 780. Without a solid foundation sitting on bedrock, the building can't get very tall or it will crumble.

Relating this back to taking a trip to California, the person who sponsored 130 was in first gear too many times. Even if they all sponsored five, he would never get out of second gear!

Learn these Napkin Presentations and use them! You won't get stuck in second gear; you'll reach high gear! Build your foundation deep, down to bedrock.

When we get to Napkin Presentation #9 (chapter ten) on motivation and attitude, you will thoroughly understand why it's important to build deep.

Before going to Napkin Presentation #5, I want to remind you that you will want to show these first four presentations to your people as soon as possible. The ones that follow can be introduced any time after your people have started sponsoring others into the business.

Notes

Chapter VI

Napkin Presentation #5
"Ships at Sea"

You have now been in your business for about a week, two weeks, a month, or whatever length of time it takes for you to decide to get serious and get growing. By this time, you have sponsored a number of people.

This presentation is one that is fun to do with a group of people, more so than in a one-on-one situation.

Almost everybody has heard the phrase, "When my ship comes in…" I'm reminded of the pessimist who flippantly quips, "With my luck, when my ship comes in, I'll be at the bus station or the airport."

In network marketing, you really can have your ship come in! If you learn and apply these Napkin Presentations, you can be there when it comes in.

I sometimes ask people if they have a long-lost relative who is going to die and leave them a lot of money. The fact is that most people really don't have much of a chance of that happening. Most people really don't have much of a chance of their ship coming in; however, in network marketing, they can!

This is just one of the reasons why I am excited about network marketing. When you're out talking to people, you can give them hope—hope that they don't have to spend the next thirty to forty years working for a company just so they can draw a pension and retire. Did you ever notice how people work thirty to forty years so they can retire and "see the world"—and now they are trying to live on half their income?

Network marketing really does give people the opportunity to see their dreams come true, and they don't have to wait or work thirty or forty years to see them.

Most people are fearful about trying to start and build a business of their own. Network marketing gives them the opportunity, without disturbing their present means of support, to get involved and try it out.

What we will show you now is how you can make your ship come in. This would represent your reaching the top of whatever network marketing organization you happen to be involved with.

When your ship arrives, you are going to "cash in" on whatever cargo it is carrying.

What we do when showing this analogy to someone is draw three ships at sea. Off to the side or at the bottom of your napkin, you draw the "shore"—that's where you are waiting for your ship to come in. Label the first ship "GOLD," the second ship "SILVER," and the third ship "M.T." (empty).

The ships represent the people in your organization whether or not you sponsored them directly. They may be at any level on down the sponsorship line(s).

Knowing that you are going to "cash in" on the cargo when your ship comes in, which of the ships are you going to work with to help it reach the shore? The Gold ship, you say? Of course! So why is it that most people seem to want to work with the M.T. ship? Because most people have never been involved in anything like this before.

The parallel is this: The Gold ships are the sales types you've sponsored and left on their own, thinking they don't need any help or direction—they are just going to run with it and really go. Maybe they will, but probably they won't—not without the success keys of building in depth rather than width.

The M.T. ships are the ones that have been in the program several months and you still have to convince them every time you see them that it will work. They tend to be somewhat negative and easily discouraged.

Most people will work with the M.T. ship—until they see this presentation. When they understand it, they will start working with the Gold ships.

When you sponsor someone into the business, he comes in as a Silver ship. It's basically determined by how you work with him whether his cargo turns to gold or becomes empty.

When we were talking about your five serious people in the first presentation, we were talking about five Gold ships. Simply put, the more Silver ships you have that turn to Gold, the fewer you have to sponsor to get your five serious people.

Here is how you can identify a Gold ship, or serious person:

1) He is EAGER TO LEARN. He calls you all the time with many questions he wants answered.

2) He ASKS FOR HELP. He has someone he wants you to see with him to sponsor or train.

3) He is EXCITED ABOUT THE BUSINESS. He understands enough about the program to know it will work, and it excites him!

4) He is making a COMMITMENT. He is buying and using the products, and he is spending his spare time learning all he can about the products and the business opportunity.

5) He has GOALS. Goals help to drive a person to get what he really wants. It's not absolutely necessary to have them written down (but it doesn't hurt), just so long as you have some definite things in mind that are a burning desire for you to achieve.

6) He has a LIST OF NAMES. That list will be written down. The reason for having it written down is simple: You can add to it at any time and you won't forget the name later. You may be driving in an area that you haven't been in for a while. Just being there will usually jog your memory of someone who lives or used to live in that neighborhood. Since you always (right?) have your list of names with you, you can immediately add his or her name to your list. A few days later when you are thinking about calling someone, you can scan down your list, and low and behold, there is that name! If you hadn't written it down when you thought of it, you may have never thought of that person again.

7) He is FUN TO BE WITH. He looks forward to your coming for a visit, business or pleasure.

8) He is POSITIVE. We all like to be around positive-thinking people—it's contagious!

The list could go on and on about the identification of a Gold ship.

Basically, the only difference between a Silver ship and a Gold one is the Silver hasn't been in the business long enough to understand it to the point of really getting serious about it.

I want you to be aware of three important words. If you just understood these three words, you would understand what makes all network marketing programs work. These words are:

#1 EXPOSE

#2 INVOLVE

#3 UPGRADE

The first thing you have to do is EXPOSE the person to the business you are in. Once you have exposed him to it, get him INVOLVED.

Once he is involved, he will be thinking about how far he can go in the program and will be UPGRADED constantly.

Expose him to network marketing by explaining the various methods (retail, direct sales, network marketing) of moving products and show him the "2 x 2 = 4" Napkin Presentation #1 (chapter two).

Get him involved. Take him on a trip to California via Napkin Presentation #3 (chapter four).

UPGRADING will be natural for him once he understands and utilizes all ten of the Napkin Presentations and sets his sights on the top.

It is very important when you phone or visit your people that they realize you are calling because you want to help them, and not think you are pushing them.

Now back to the M.T. (empty) ship type of people. When you call them because you want to help them, you get the feeling that they aren't exactly thrilled about your calling. This is a very good indication that they feel you are being "pushy" and bugging them. When you call M.T. ships, they think you are pressuring them.

On the other hand, when you call Gold ships, they just figure that you are calling because you want to help, and you will pick that up in the tone of their conversation.

M.T. ships don't have goals, they don't have a list of names, they are definitely not serious, and on top of all that they're usually a little bit negative. They are the ones you must keep proving things to all the time.

Realize that when the M.T. ship sinks, it will either go down alone, or in the event that you work with an M.T. ship rather than a Gold, it will drag you down with it. That is why we try to train our people to stay away from the M.T. ships and work with the Gold ships, or with the Silvers to help them become Gold ships. Spend most of your time working with the Gold ships to develop their own organizations down-group.

All of a sudden, the M.T.s who haven't sunk (i.e., dropped from the program) and the Silvers who haven't converted to Gold yet will see you moving ahead without them, and they just might call you instead. If a person's attitude about the business is on the way down, trying to stop it en route is next to impossible—you almost have to let it hit bottom. Then when he is ready and he calls you and wants to get together and get going and get growing, you can bring him up very quickly. But if you run the risk of trying to bring him up while he's on the way down (i.e., working with a sinking ship, an empty one at that), he very likely could drag you down with him.

This is somewhat of an enjoyable way of communicating with your distributors. When you get together, you can ask them how they are doing with their ships; how many Golds? how many Silvers? etc.

Important point: Never ever call up a new distributor and ask him how much he sold last week! If you do, you have totally invalidated everything you've told him, because you told him right up front that he didn't have to go out and sell.

He is just going to share with his friends, sponsor, and build an organization.

If you ask him what he's sold, his first reaction will be to think that you are only interested in knowing how much money you are going to make off of him—and he is probably thinking correctly.

The money will come automatically if you seek first to help your people succeed. Zig Ziglar puts it this way: "You can have anything in the world that you want, simply by helping enough other people to get what they want."

When you want to talk to someone in your organization that you sponsored directly, whenever possible, call someone down-line from him and chat with him a little to see if there is anyone you can help him meet with or talk to. Afterward, you can call the first-level person you originally wanted to talk to, and the first thing you let him know is that you were just talking with one of his distributors who is excited and that you are going to get together with him.

Display to your people that when you call, you are calling to help them, not to check up on them.

Checking up on people is the direct sales company's sales manager's job, not yours. We are not in direct sales—we are in network marketing. By now you should be aware of the difference.

To wrap up this presentation, we point out that you the reader are not an M.T. ship. If you are, you probably wouldn't be reading this book. If you feel you were an M.T. ship before you began to read this book, by the time you get this far you are probably a Gold, or at least a Silver well on your way to becoming a Gold ship. Keep it up!

Chapter VII

Napkin Presentation #6
"Third-Party Invitation"

Prospecting is the subject of this presentation, which is actually tied in with the "Ships at Sea" presentation. More simply, we call prospecting the Third-Party Invitation. It's important that all your people know what a Third-Party Invitation is and how to do it.

Explanation: If I know Carol, I do not go up and ask Carol if she's interested in earning some extra income. The reason I don't do that is because even if Carol wanted (or even needed) to earn some extra money, she would probably want me to think that she's doing okay financially and would say, "No, I'm really not interested."

What I do is go up to Carol and say something that sounds like, "Carol, I got started in a new exciting business, and you might be able to help me. Would you happen to know anyone who would be interested in earning some extra income?" (or "interested in getting into a second business?").

Notice the "Third Party": anyone. I'm asking her if she knows anyone.

Do a little experimenting on this. The next ten people you run into (gas station attendant, grocer, barber, cleaners, etc.), ask them if they know anybody who'd like to earn some extra income, just to get their reaction. Their response will tell you something.

Most of the time, their response will probably be, "What is it?" The reason they say, "What is it?" is because the person they know who would like to earn some extra income is themselves—they just want to know a little more about it so they can make a decision.

When they say, "What is it?" don't give them the big curiosity shot. Some people are offended by getting dragged off to somebody's home for an hour-and-a-half presentation when they have no idea why they are going there. (Some companies train their people to not say anything.) Your reply when they ask you what it is will be, "Do you know anything about network marketing?" They will either say yes or no. If they say yes, ask them what they know about it. Get into a general discussion with them about network marketing. (Refer to chapter one, "Introduction to Network Marketing.") Point out some of the features and benefits of being involved in network marketing in general.

From there, invite them to sit down with you (if they're still interested) to take a look at the particular program that you're in. Explain to them that it would take only an hour or so to tell them the whole story. Don't try to "shotgun" the program to them on a street corner or while they are supposed to be working. Without the whole story you'd just be confusing them—just enough confusing information for them to say no, and not enough information for them to say yes.

If you follow the training of your people the way it's laid out for you, you won't have to prospect. In the process of helping the people that you brought into the business, you will run into other people that you will be able to talk to. When you run into these people, you want to talk to them about network marketing so you can introduce them to your program. Most people have some fears about doing that. Where those fears come from is the idea that the person will say no to them. It's called the "fear of rejection."

A good example would be at a high-school dance. A guy is at the first dance he's ever been to. He walks clear across the room and asks a girl to dance, and she says no. So he turns around, rejected, and walks back, never again to ask a girl to dance. He will absolutely swear that everybody in the whole auditorium saw him get rejected. Nobody likes to be rejected.

Another type will ask a girl to dance, and if she says no, will ask the next girl and the next ... and that fellow will be dancing all night.

To overcome the fear of rejection, we want you to be able to trick your mind so you will be able to talk to more people. To do that, picture yourself standing on a dock. Remember, if you are waiting for your ship to come in, you'll have had to already have sent your ship(s) out.

You have to launch some ships. If you launched only one ship and it returned empty, what good did it do to have your ship "come in" at all? The more ships you launch, the better chance you will have of some of them coming in carrying gold. The ships carrying gold are the ones you should work with.

Most people have never launched a ship, so there's nothing already in your subconscious that can hurt you. Notice the launching ramp. When you ask someone if he knows anybody who would like to earn some extra income, you have just launched a ship. If he says, "No, I don't know anybody," you can say, "Fine. If you happen to run into anybody, would you have them call me?" (Give him your card.) So you weren't rejected.

There are only two possible results in launching a ship. It will either float, or it will sink.

If it sinks, so what! You're standing on the dock!

If it floats, great! Send it out and help it to turn into a gold-carrying vessel.

After presenting the Napkin Presentations #5 and #6, people will tell you they plan on being a "Gold." The reason they tell you that is because you have just told them that you only work with the Gold ships, and they want you to work with them. Take advantage of their invitation—you will benefit also!

Notes

Chapter VIII

Napkin Presentation #7
"Where to Spend Your Time"

Below is a graph that lays out pictorially where you should be spending your time. Basically, 100 percent of your time at the beginning should be spent sponsoring people.

"But," you ask, "should I not be spending my time learning, as the first few weeks are supposed to be my training month?" You are correct. But remember, your sponsor, helping you to sponsor, *is* part of your training. Even though your sponsor does the "work," you still get credit for being the sponsor.

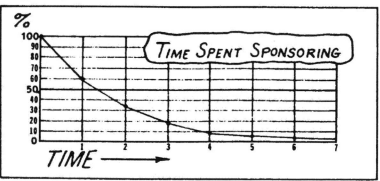

In network marketing programs, you can sponsor someone else into the business just as soon as you have been sponsored.

When you first get into network marketing, your business is YOU. If you want your business to be a successful business, you now know that you must find five serious people to sponsor. You may have to sponsor more than five to find five that want to be serious.

As time goes on, the amount of time you spend on sponsoring people drops off. Why? Because all of a sudden you find one serious person ... then two serious people ... then three ... four ... and when you have five serious people, you can quit spending your time looking for people to sponsor. Spend your time teaching those five Gold ships to sponsor. Teach them also to teach their people to sponsor. When they have gone three or four deep in building their own groups and don't need you anymore, then you can go looking for another serious person to sponsor to replace them.

When you have five serious people, you should be spending 95 percent of your time working with them, 2.5 percent of your time servicing the customers you have from your friends, and 2.5 percent of your time "planting seeds." This way, when one or more of your five serious people are "harvested" and don't need to be "watered and cultivated" anymore, you can work with the "seeds" you planted and help them to "sprout."

You should be aware that 100 percent of the time, you are moving the product. It's a natural result of working with your people. That's the "selling" part of the business, which we like to call the "sharing" part.

Notes

Chapter IX

Napkin Presentation #8
"The Sizzle Sells the Steak"

Another title that we sometimes use for this presentation is "The Blazes." I assume you have been camping. You will notice that if you separate the logs of a campfire, the fire will go out. If you put them back together again, the fire will blaze up. So if you have one log, you have nothing.

If you have two logs, you'll have a flame.

When you put three logs together, you will have a fire.

By the time you put together four logs, you'll have a blaze!

People are the same way. The next time you're meeting someone with your sponsor, in a restaurant for example, and arrive first (being there by yourself), notice how much energy there is (or isn't) around the table.

Notice when your sponsor arrives and there are two of you, how there is much more energy!

The two of you are there to meet with someone, and when he arrives, there is even more energy.

When the fourth person arrives, you've really got it going! We like to call these "blazes" or "Sizzle Sessions." Your network marketing program is the "steak," and everybody knows that the sizzle sells the steak!

So you want to get together with your sponsor and share the Napkin Presentations with one or two of your down-line people and get them "sizzling" and excited about what can happen.

A good place to do this is in a restaurant. Pick a time when the restaurant is the least busy, around 10 a.m. or 2 p.m. You may want to set up a schedule so your people will know where you'll be at various times during the week. It's as if everybody's out gathering wood for the fire or blaze.

If you were to bring someone to a Sizzle Session who was a little bit skeptical (a "wet log") and introduce him to the blaze, he would dry out and become part of the fire.

So what happens if you are all by yourself and you, being new in the business, talk to someone who is skeptical? That's like trying to put a wet log on nothing.

Let's say you are a twig, just getting started in the business. Your sponsor, who's been around a little longer, is a log. A log and a twig can create a flame. Just having someone with you can make a difference. It gives your sponsor someone to bounce conversation off of. I could want Joe to get a message, and if I'm talking to him directly, he might not really "hear" what  I'm saying. But if I'm talking to Carol, knowing that Joe is listening… It's amazing how people get more out of conversations they "listen in" on than if someone were talking to them directly.

Another thing about these blazes in a restaurant: They get very energetic! There are people (called "eavesdroppers") who could be "listening in" on some of our conversation. You can spot them, leaning back, trying to hear more, etc. Be aware, some of these people will be very interested. When you're all done with your Sizzle Session and start to break up, stick around a few more minutes. Give the eavesdroppers an opportunity to approach you. They won't come over to the table when there are four people there, but they may come over if you are by yourself.

We always start the "blazing" sessions by having the people, as they arrive, tell something positive that has happened with the products or their organization. While we're there, we talk only about the business. We don't try to solve the Middle East crisis or any of the world's other problems. We are there to share ideas about how to build our business and how to talk to people about our business.

We always break up our sessions with a parting word that goes something like, "Just think! This is as hard as we will ever work!" This gets a little contagious, especially if you have people join your group who still have their regular nine-to-five job and have to leave because their "lunch hour" is gone. You might say to them as they leave to go back to work, "See you later, Nick, but remember…" He may interrupt with, "Yeah, I know. That's as hard as you'll ever work." Nick will be motivated to hurry up and get to that same position.

Notes

Notes

Chapter X

Napkin Presentation #9
"Motivation and Attitude"

One of the most important of the Napkin Presentations is this one on motivation. This will give you an excellent understanding of what motivates people. You will learn how to work with your people to motivate them.

MOTIVATION

DOWN | UP
"Hot Bath" | "Constant"

Start out by writing the word "motivation" at the top of your napkin or board.

You next draw two arrows—one pointing down, and the other pointing up. Point out that there are two kinds of motivation: Down Motivation and Up Motivation—label the arrows. Down Motivation is what we call "hot bath," but Up Motivation is constant. Let me explain. Most of you probably have been to rah-rah motivational rallies and found yourself gung-ho to get with it and get going (again) with the program you are in. You usually find that you've cooled off again in a couple of weeks or months. When you take a hot bath, it seems the hotter the bath, the quicker you cool off.

I have seen people go to motivational rallies that last up to three days—then two weeks after they get home, they are totally depressed. Why? For three days they get hyped up, really motivated, but nobody told them what to do and/or how to do it! That's why they get down.

Even reading this book is "hot bath." (I'll get to Up Motivation in a little bit.) Going to seminars, getting together with your sponsor, reading a book, moving some product, obtaining more knowledge—these are all forms of hot-bath motivation, or Down Motivation. That's not to say they are bad—for they are necessary.

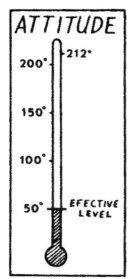

Before I talk about Up Motivation, I want to talk about attitude. Imagine that you are going to talk to someone about your business. That person doesn't know anything about it, so he has an attitude level of zero. Let's say for you to be effective in talking to him about the business, you need an attitude level of 50 degrees. If your attitude level is short of 50 degrees, don't talk to anybody, because they will just drag you down.

The person you want to sponsor has come to your presentation. He has signed the application. He wants to get started—and, boy, is he excited about the business! He's all the way up to 65 degrees—he's going to get rich! Before he has had a chance to learn anything, he goes out and starts talking to people. Since he really doesn't know how to handle himself when confronted by negative skeptics, he becomes negative himself. These skeptics may even be well-meaning relatives and friends who may have been disillusioned by getting "signed up" by someone who just wanted to "get rich" off of them, rather than by someone who was willing or able to help them build a business—a real "sponsor"—with a commitment to helping others ahead of helping himself.

What will happen is that he will drop below the 50-degree level. You get back together with him again, answer the objections and questions he may have, and he'll go back up, maybe to 70 degrees. And this time, he will stay up a little bit longer before he goes below 50 degrees again in his attitude level.

The question: How would you like to have an attitude level of about 50 degrees all the time? In other words, you aren't up and down like a yo-yo but constant. The only way we know of that you can do this is with Up Motivation—because Up Motivation is constant.

Here is Up Motivation. You have a sponsor. Your sponsor (SP) will help to sponsor people for you. We start with five. Notice that when you sponsor five people, you have only 25 degrees. Again, a mistake to avoid is sponsoring more than you can effectively work with, adding 5 degrees at a time and losing them just as fast.

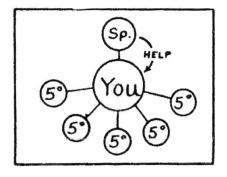

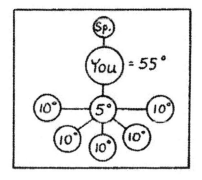

Your sponsor helped you sponsor these five people, and you in turn will help these five people sponsor others for their 5 degrees. Their 5 degrees is 10 degrees for you. All your second-level people are worth 10 degrees each for you. Notice: If you only helped one of the five people sponsor five others, that would put you above 50 degrees.

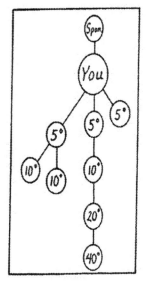

Notice what happens when you teach sponsoring down another level. The third level is 20 degrees. The fourth is 40 degrees. The deeper you go, the hotter it gets!

The only time you can appreciate this phenomenon is when it's first happening—and that's why you want it to happen to your people as soon as it can possibly happen to them. Once they experience it, they will be excited!

Here is an example:

Carol sponsors Tom, and Tom sponsors Bill. Carol gets a phone call and finds out that Bill went out last week and sponsored five serious people—he's really going to run with it! What happens is, that excites everybody right up the sponsorship line. Note the arrow going up. That's why we call it "Up Motivation."

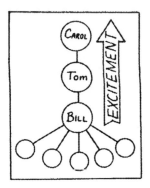

You need to help the people you sponsored support their people. Let me show you an exception to that. When you sponsor someone into the business, he is a Silver ship. Everyone comes in as a Silver. They're excited, but they haven't gotten serious yet.

Everybody has at least one friend. Get together with your people—help them to sponsor some of their friends who come in as Silver ships. Support your people as they help their friends to sponsor more friends on down-line three or more deep. All of a sudden, down-line there somewhere, you will find someone who turns out to be a Gold ship. Here is what you do: Go down and work with that Gold, the first real Gold you have in that line. What will happen is that in the process of helping the Gold, the Silvers will be converted to Gold.

That is how you convert the Silvers; get someone under them. If that person under them really goes (is a Gold), the Silver who sponsored him will say, "Hey! I'd better get my act together!" There isn't anything that will motivate people more than to have someone under them doing something. It has been said, "You can motivate people faster and more effectively by putting a candle under their sitting place than by putting a blowtorch to their thinking place."

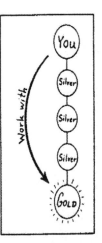

To wrap this up: The one thing you don't want to do is develop a dependency to you on the part of your people, the ones you sponsored. They cannot be dependent on you forever; otherwise, it's not going to work. There has to be a point where they don't need you. We say that this point is when your people can teach their people to teach all ten of

the Napkin Presentations; then they know everything they need to know to build a strong organization. Then you can go find another serious person to replace them.

Let's suppose, for this example, you sponsored Sue. You would say, "Sue, let's say you are like the sun. The sun has more energy than anything we know of." (It is kind of an indirect compliment.) You continue by saying, "The person you sponsor is like a pan of water." (Note: You sponsored Sue, but don't assume the role of the sun and call her a pan of water—it's not that flattering.)

So, in your group there is a "sun." At what point would the water boil? If you took a pan of water and set it out in the middle of the hottest desert on the hottest day of the year, it still would not boil. It will take 212 degrees for the water to begin to boil. It won't boil at 210 degrees or 211 degrees; it has to be at least 212 degrees to boil.

So take note: If your attitude is at 212 degrees, and only needs to be at 50 degrees to be effective, you could talk to anybody at any time about what you're doing. So that's the direction your attitude is heading. We just told you that the sun can't make the water boil— your sponsor can't make the water boil either. None of the "hot bath" motivation can.

I don't care if all the top people in all of the network marketing companies came to town for a rally and you went to all of them—your water will not boil. They can get your attitude above the 50-degree effective level, but it's up to you to get the water boiling. And remember, your sponsor will help you.

In other words, you know some people your sponsor doesn't know. Your sponsor will go with you and help

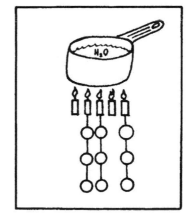

you to sponsor someone. Once you have sponsored someone, you have started the burner under the pan. With five people sponsored, you now have the pan sitting on five jets of the burner, the maximum number the pan can effectively cover. Notice: The water isn't boiling yet; it's only 25 degrees if your five people have not sponsored anyone yet. But, if any three run off a string three deep, or any two a string four deep, or any one a string five deep, the water begins to boil. Any combination that adds up to 212 under the pan will get the water to boil. At the time the water is boiling, the sun (sponsor) can go away and the water will continue to boil. Once you've shown a person this, and you call him on the phone, he realizes that you are calling because you want to help him. You are not calling to give him a blowtorch to the head, but rather you are calling to see if you can light another burner or turn the temperature up on those already lit. You want to help him get his

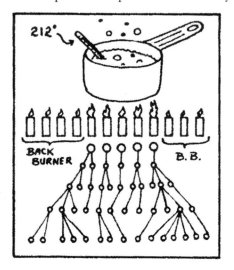

water to boil. The farther you go down the group, the hotter the burner gets.

Once you have a person with his water boiling, it may look similar to the example to the left. Notice that you have sponsored others as well. The first one to boil is not necessarily the first one you sponsored. It is the first one that got serious and got the depth in his organization to get and keep it going.

When the water boils there, you can continue working with five serious people. Notice that the pan can sit on only five burners at a time. (This kind of goes along with the first presentation in chapter two.) If you have fifteen people sponsored into the business, you can really work effectively with but five at a time. You may have to sponsor ten to twenty people to get those five serious people. What happens to the others? We put them on the back burner, so to speak.

So, when you have the water boiling on one or more of the "five," before you go out to search for someone brand new to sponsor, take a trip around the back burner and let them know what's going on. You may find that because of timing and circumstances at the time you sponsored them, they weren't ready yet to get serious about the business, but they are ready now. Maybe they were just waiting to see how the program was going to work for you. So take a trip around the back burner.

Notes

Notes

Chapter XI

Napkin Presentation #10
"Pentagon of Growth"

Five has been the magic number throughout this book, so it's only appropriate that this final presentation is a five-sided fun trip of a mathematical exercise, which also tends to be a motivator every time you show it to someone.

This "Pentagon of Growth" lays out an important view of how fast your organization can grow, if you adopt the principles that we have outlined in this book.

You start by drawing a pentagon and writing "You" in the middle of it. We'll allow for a training month and use increments of two months as we develop the growth of our organization. (You can use whatever time frame you wish, however.)

You come into the business and in two months you have sponsored five people who really want to get a handle on life. (Write "2M-5" by one side of the pentagon as shown in the figure for "2 Months.")

In two more months (i.e., at the end of four months), the five from the second month, having been taught to do what you're doing, give you twenty-five second-level distributors. At the same time, you have developed five more serious first-level people. Your pentagon is now looking like the one above.

After six months, you may have 125 third-level people under your "original" five, twenty-five second-levels under your second group of five serious people, plus you have developed a third set of five.

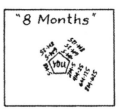

At the end of eight months, your pentagon of growth may appear like the example to the right.

Now at this point, hand the napkin (or board) over to your student, give him the pen, and have

him complete the diagram on out for ten months. Just put a line for ten months (10M ____) of the original group as the figure is too large to effectively identify with; it's over 3,000 (3,125 to be exact). The example to the left is what he should now have.

Go around the pentagon one more time and extend it to a year.

To really put emphasis on how building in depth can make your organization grow rapidly, cross out all of the groups except the one under your original five serious people. Point out to the person you are showing this to that if all he built was this one group (and he didn't do any of the ones crossed out), he would be making $6,000 per month or more—depending on the "vehicle" he was using. The main purpose of this exercise is to simply show the importance of working down-group with the people that you sponsor—and to teach them to do the same. **Now go do it!**

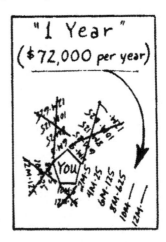

Chapter XII

Going Back to School

Your attitude can make a big difference when you are trying to sponsor a new distributor. Most distributors seem to have the attitude of, "Who can I get into my business?" I think the proper attitude is, "To whom will I next offer the opportunity to retire?" If you believed a person could retire in one to three years and you understood how to present this possibility in a presentation that takes only two minutes, why would you want to give this opportunity to a stranger?

To be able to retire in one to three years at better than $50,000 per year, a person must be willing to go back to school. He can learn everything he would need to know by investing five to ten hours per week for six months. "Retiring" simply means "not going to work unless you want to." If someone tells you he will give it thirty days to see how it goes, don't waste your time. You can't dig your foundation in thirty days. It takes at least six months.

The school I am referring to is a school of involvement. From the time you leave your home for your weekly training session, attend the meeting, have coffee and drive home, you have already spent three to five hours. The rest of the time is spent listening to positive motivational tapes and tapes about your program, meeting with your sponsor, attending Sizzle Sessions, talking to prospects, etc. This can all be done along with anything else you have already been doing outside of network marketing.

While doing seminars, I have asked this question all across the United States and Canada: "Does anyone know of a four-year college course where you could graduate then hope to retire in one to three years at better than $50,000 per year?" I have never had anyone tell me of one. No one anywhere can come up with a college course where that is even a remote possibility. That is what is exciting about network marketing. You can actually learn in six months everything you need to know to retire in one to three years.

Do you remember when you were in college and you went to the bookstore and bought your books for the quarter? Big, heavy, thick textbooks. You could hardly wait to get back to your room so you could start studying them. Do you remember how you could hardly wait until the end of the quarter to be tested on the material? While you were going to school, did anyone pay you for going? Since you went to college for four years without getting paid and since you had no hope of retiring in one to three years, then why do you get so concerned about how little you have made in your first few months in network marketing? Remember, you are in school. Network marketing school.

Some people in network marketing get discouraged after only a few weeks. I don't think they have a right to be discouraged unless they have had at least six months of network marketing school. Try letting a medical student operate on you after he has been in school for a few weeks. You would probably be very disappointed with the outcome.

Ask a doctor, a lawyer, a dentist, or any other professional person how long he has been practicing his profession. His answer will be figured from the time he graduated, not from his first day as a college freshman. When you ask someone in network marketing how long he has been in the business, he will tell you from the day he first signed his Distributor Agreement or Application. You should actually keep track of the time you are in the network marketing business beginning from the time when you knew what you were doing.

The only time you will be disappointed is when you expect something and you don't get it or it doesn't happen. Too many distributors come into network marketing expecting to start making big money right away. First and foremost, you need to go to school. That will take at least six months. Consider those going to college. After six months into their freshman year, they still have three and a half years to go before they are even ready to look for a job.

To be really successful in network marketing, you must teach someone else to be successful. Your distributors need to quit being so concerned about what kind of money they are making and increase their concern for teaching and working with their down-line. The quicker they do this, the quicker they will find real success in network marketing. But this takes time. Before you can teach others, you first must learn what to do yourself.

If you have distributors in your organization who have trouble talking to their friends, it's probably because they really don't believe they could retire in one to three years, or they don't understand how they could actually make it happen. The following is a simple presentation you can use to show how someone could build a large income in six months to three years. It only takes a few minutes to learn and about two minutes to make the presentation. It is a variation taken from Napkin Presentation #1 in chapter two.

Let's assume that you have a new distributor to whom you say, "With all of the people you know or could meet with my help, do you think you could sponsor five people by the end of your first month? People who would like to learn how to retire in one to three years?"

Most people will say, "Everyone I know would like to be able to do that."

Don't make the mistake of going with your distributor to see five people at one time. Go with your distributor five times to see each person individually. If you see all five at once, one negative person could spoil it for the other four. Besides, if you go with your distributor five times, your distributor will get to see the presentation five times rather than only once. Now with this training, he will be ready to go with each of his distributors five times. Your distributor will become an expert by practicing on his distributor's prospects just as you have become an expert by practicing on his prospects.

If you can sponsor five serious distributors by the end of your first thirty days, you should be able to help them sponsor five by the end of three months. When your distributors are helping their five, you are now supporting down-group and teaching your people to do the same.

You should be at the third level by the end of six months. So what if it took a year? When making this presentation, the lines on either side of the 5, 25, and 125 represent your wholesale buyers or the people who signed up to get you off their backs. Your presentation should look like this:

$$— You —$$

$$End\ of\ 1^{st}Mo.\ —5—$$
$$End\ of\ 3^{rd}Mo.\ —25—$$
$$End\ of\ 6^{th}Mo.\ —125—$$

At this point, you would have a total of 155 serious distributors.

If you are building your business right, in the process of sharing your opportunity, you will have some who will not take advantage of it. Many of these will become either a wholesale buyer or a retail customer.

Let us say that each of your distributors down-line has at least ten friend-customers. When you multiply ten friend-customers by 155 serious distributors, you would have 1,550 friend-customers. Since your distributors are also customers, you need to add 155 to 1,550, giving you a total customer count of 1,705. Also consider that there are three reasons why a distributor-customer will purchase more products than a friend-customer: 1) The distributor-customer is more familiar with the entire line of products; 2) The distributor-customer can buy the products wholesale and is more likely to be generous with his use personally; 3) The distributor-customer buys products to give away as samples. You should encourage all of your distributors to use samples as well as use samples yourself.

The line under the "155" represents your wholesale buyers, which we are not counting. This would only mean a plus. Your presentation at this point would look something like this:

```
        — You —          155 Serious Distrib.
End of 1ˢᵗ Mo. —5—      x 10 Friend Customers
End of 3ʳᵈ Mo. —25—      1550    "        "
End of 6ᵗʰ Mo. —125—    +155 Distrib.    "
                        - - - - - Wholesale Buyers
                         1705 Total Customers
```

Now multiply the 1,705 by $30 to get total group sales per month. Most of you are in programs where your personal sales are much more than $30 per month. I use this figure to be a little conservative. You don't want to completely blow your prospect's mind. That is why at level three you ask, "What if it took a year instead of six months? Would it be worth it?"

When you multiply $30 by 1,705 total customers, you come up with $51,150 total volume. Point out that you are only working with just five serious distributors.

With a volume of over $50,000 per month in sales, not counting your wholesale buyers, you should be making somewhere between $2,000 and $6,000 per month.

The reason for the spread between $2,000 and $6,000 per month is that everyone may not have their ten friend-customers; some may have more.

At this point, you should be ten to fifteen minutes into your presentation. This is when you ask the question that lets you know if your prospect is willing to take the time to learn how to drive. If he says no, go right to the products and get another retail customer. If he says yes, go to the next presentation, the difference between five and six. When you complete this presentation, he will be more than ready to check out your vehicle.

**Here is the $64 question: If you could be making $2,000 to
$6,000 per month in six months on top of what you are currently
earning, could you see yourself going back to school for five to ten
hours per week for six months to learn how to do it?**

This presentation is simple and it explains the mechanics of how an
organization can grow. It is a combination of building the organization
and everyone retailing a minimum amount. Anyone can build ten
friend-customers. It doesn't take a salesperson to do this. When
completed, your entire presentation should look like this:

$$
\begin{array}{ll}
\multicolumn{2}{c}{-You-}\\[4pt]
\text{End of } 1^{ST} \text{ Mo. } -5- & 155 \text{ Serious Distrib.}\\
\text{End of } 3^{rd} \text{ Mo. } -25- & \times 10 \text{ Friend Customers}\\
\text{End of } 6^{th} \text{ Mo. } -125- & 1550 \quad '' \qquad ''\\
\text{(or Year)} & +155 \text{ Distrib. } \quad ''\\
& ----- \text{ Wholesale Buyers}\\
& 1705 \text{ Total Customers}\\
& \times \$30\\
& \$51,150 \text{ Total Volume}
\end{array}
$$

The meaning of a "serious" distributor in this presentation is a
distributor who has made the following commitment: He will get
involved for a minimum of five to ten hours per week for at least six
months. This is the only way he can learn the business.

Chapter XIII

Playing with Numbers to Make a Point

So what do you do when one of your front-liners (personally sponsored distributors) reaches the point where he doesn't need you anymore? (Refer to Napkin Presentation #9, chapter ten.) You are now free to sponsor someone else and work a new line. The definition of a "line" is when your distributor's organization is at least three levels deep.

Instead of wondering who you are going to bring into your business, you now get to make a choice. Out of all the people you have met while working down-group with your first five serious distributors, you now get to select one who will have an opportunity for early retirement.

It is exciting to realize that you can select someone who will get this opportunity. You carry a lot of power when you totally understand and believe.

Now you have six serious distributors in your front line. Point out the difference between five and six, which is, of course, one. Continue down-group. Six times six equals thirty-six. Five times five equals twenty-five. The difference between thirty-six and twenty-five is eleven. Do it one more time. Five times twenty-five is 125. Six times thirty-six is 216, and the difference between 216 and 125 is ninety-one. Your presentation at this point should now look something like this:

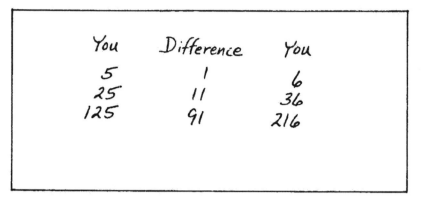

All programs that have breakaways will pay well beyond five levels and most uni-level programs will pay down seven levels. Continue downline with the multiples of five to the seventh level. Your presentation should now look like this:

You	Difference	You
5	1	6
25	11	36
125	91	216
625		
3,125		
15,625		
78,125		

This presentation is easy to learn. Notice that when you get to 125 in the level column, the last three digits alternate between 125 and 625. This would continue no matter how many levels you go down. So all you have to remember is three, fifteen, and seventy-eight.

At this point in the presentation, you suggest to your distributor that he complete the calculations on his own. In other words, multiply 216 by six (which is 1,296) and subtract 625 from it. That is a difference of 671. Continue this process down to the seventh level. The impact will be much greater if you have him do it himself.

Ask this question: "What do you think the answer will be at the seventh level?" Let him guess. Most people will not even come close. The difference at the seventh level is over 200,000 (201,811 to be precise)! Your presentation should now look like this:

You	Difference	You
5	1	6
25	11	36
125	91	216
625	?	—
3,125	?	—
15,625	?	—
78,125	201,811	—

Obviously, 201,811 is quite a difference. You should mention to your distributor that once someone understands this, he can see the importance of working down-group. Why be concerned with having so many in your front line? You couldn't work with them anyway. Besides, sponsoring too many in your front line gets you involved in a game we call "adding and subtracting." I would much rather play the game of multiplication called network marketing.

All you have to do to play this game is teach your people three deep. When you teach three deep, you will actually end up five deep. For example: My name is Don, and I sponsor Steve. I say to Steve, "When getting a new person started, the most important thing you can teach him is to make sure when he sponsors someone, get that person three deep as soon as possible."

Before he even knows about it, this will automatically bring Napkin Presentation #9 on motivation into play.

Steve is a good student. When he sponsors Pam, he helps her and supports her down-line, making sure she works three deep. This is a variation of Napkin Presentation #2 and should look like this:

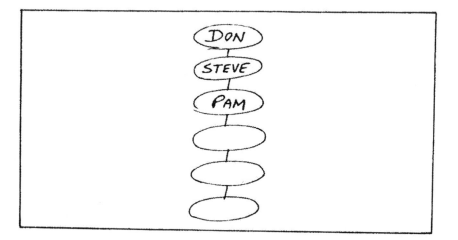

Now count the depth. You have five levels below you. You taught Steve to make sure his people are three deep. Steve will now teach his people what you taught him and you will go even deeper. Can you see now why teachers do so well in network marketing?

Most "salesmen," when they get started building an organization, think it is a sponsor, sponsor, and sponsor business. Actually, what it is, is a sponsor and teach, sponsor and teach, sponsor and teach business. You will never make it in network marketing until you teach someone else how to make it.

If you continue your presentation showing the difference between five and six to the fourth level, you would have 1,296 minus 625 for a difference of 671. The total of the differences through the first four levels would be 774. Your total distributors on the left side would be 780, and the total on the right side would be 1,554. Your presentation would look like this:

You	Difference	You
5	1	6
25	11	36
125	91	216
625	671	1296
Totals 780	774	1554

You are now on your own. Multiply 780 or 1,554 by ten friend-customers. Add the friend-customers to the distributor-customers. Now multiply this total by $30 per month and then multiply the result by twelve months. Remember, I am not even considering the wholesale buyers. Now can you see how one could retire in one to three years? You can't do it sponsoring wide without going deep.

This presentation is a continuation of Napkin Presentation #1.

Notes

Notes

Chapter XIV

Business Training Sessions vs. Weekly Opportunity Meetings

Most people in network marketing get their start by attending a weekly opportunity meeting. Since this is how they came into the business, they think that weekly opportunity meetings and getting people to them is what the business is all about. After they have invited so many to the meeting, they quit inviting. This is because they figure they have more than enough coming. What happens? On the night of the meeting, no one shows up. This can be very discouraging.

A typical opportunity meeting will look something like this: A room is set up with chairs in theatre style, either in a home or a hotel room. A blackboard or whiteboard is sitting on an easel up front. A person in a three-piece suit is giving a presentation about the company, the products, and of course, the marketing plan. This, in most cases, lasts for approximately one and one-half hours.

Out of twenty-two people who show up for the opportunity meeting, there will be nineteen distributors and three new guests. Most of those invited as guests didn't even show up. The person putting on the meeting is talking to the guests. He or she is talking to only three of the twenty-two people there! For the distributor who has already been to the meeting several times and seen the same presentation over and over, this becomes very boring. One tends to get what we call "meeting burnout."

During the presentation, you keep an eye on the guests and you notice positive nods when the speaker is talking about the company, products, and marketing plan. With all this positive body language, why do the guests sometimes turn down the opportunity when asked if they see themselves getting started? It doesn't make any sense that they could like everything they have seen and heard and still say no.

The reason for the no is simple. They look at the person giving the presentation as being "successful." They think that for themselves to be successful they will have to conduct meetings. Maybe not right away, but sometime they will have to conduct meetings—a thing most people fear even more than dying. They fear getting up in front of a group of people and speaking. Now you can understand why they turn down the opportunity you have offered. (By the way, that's an important point: They have said no to the opportunity, not to you personally. Don't let these "no's" discourage you.)

I prove this point while I'm doing seminars. I say, "Since I'm limited for time, I only have time to call on one person. Would the people who would like to come up and talk about anything they choose for the next three minutes please raise your hand." Very few, less than 5 percent, raise their hands. You should see the look of relief on the faces of those who did when I tell them I was only kidding.

I know hundreds of people who can carry on a conversation with a friend over a cup of coffee. These same people freak out at even the thought of getting up in front of a group. Even the size of the group doesn't make any difference. Some company presidents even break out in a cold sweat when merely getting up in front of their board of directors or making a presentation to the stockholders.

How would you like to avoid this fear when building your organization? How would you like to have exciting weekly opportunity meetings? You can. Once you understand how, your organization will grow many times faster.

We meet with our prospects one on one or at a Sizzle Session. (See chapter nine, Napkin Presentation #8.) We prefer to meet in a restaurant at an off time for the restaurant. We invite our guests to bring a tape recorder. They could use the tape to review the presentation later or as a tool to help them sponsor their friends.

I always prefer that they have read the book *How to Build a Large Successful Multi-Level Marketing Organization* prior to my meeting with them. This can save you a considerable amount of time. If they already know "how to drive" before you meet with them, it's easier to help them select a "vehicle." (Refer to Napkin Presentation #3 in chapter four.)

After some idle conversation about the benefits of network marketing, tell them you would like to give them a twenty-minute presentation about your company, products, and marketing plan. Since you announced that it only takes about twenty minutes, it points out that anyone could learn to give a twenty-minute presentation. Besides, until they learn it, all they have to do is play the tape for their friends.

If it takes you an hour and one-half to present your company, products, and marketing plan, you may become too selective about who you are making appointments with. How many one-and-one-half-hour appointments are you up to doing? When you get your presentation down to twenty minutes, you can be productive during a coffee break or make a couple of presentations during your lunch break.

I would break the twenty-minute presentation down as follows: Three minutes to talk about the company. Seven minutes to talk about the products and give them some samples. Allow about ten minutes to explain the marketing plan. Break your total marketing plan into several parts. In most cases, you will not need to explain the latter parts to get your people started. Remember, they have made a commitment to go back to school for five to ten hours a week to learn the business. During your first meeting, don't try to show them everything they will learn in the next six months.

The two most important words in network marketing are "sponsor" and "teach." The least important word is "sell." "Sell" should always be replaced with the word "share." The next three words of importance are "expose," "involve," and "upgrade." First you expose a person to your business. Then you get him involved for five to ten hours per week over the next six months. His knowledge and motivation as to where he wants to go in the business will upgrade as he goes along. He may come in thinking about making an additional $300 to $500 per month, but after being involved for six months, his thinking will probably be upgraded to making several thousand dollars on a monthly basis.

If your prospect forgets his tape recorder, have yours ready and let him keep the tape when you are finished. When you start your twenty-minute presentation, ask him to write down any questions he may have and explain that you will answer them when you are finished. Point out that if you had to answer questions during the presentation, you wouldn't be able to keep it to twenty minutes.

The tool (the tape) you are giving your new distributor gives you a valid reason for keeping your presentation orderly, without interruption every two minutes. The tape presentation will also be orderly. If you were to answer one question during your presentation, it would be like trying to let only one of several cats out of a bag. Once you start jumping around, you will lose the continuity of your presentation.

If your prospect shows any hesitation as to whether he could do the business, simply say to him, "Before you make your final decision, why don't you come to our weekly training session and see how we train our people?"

The purpose of the weekly training session is to teach your distributors how to sit down with a friend over a cup of coffee and give a twenty-minute presentation about your company, products, and marketing plan. The entire training session should not last more than one hour.

Unlike an opportunity meeting, in a weekly training session you are directing your conversation toward your distributors rather than toward the guests. Have you ever noticed how much more believable a conversation is when you are listening in on it rather than having it directed to you? While you are teaching your distributors how to present your company, products, and marketing plan, your guests are getting trained also.

The net result of this style of teaching is that you now have nineteen distributors who are better prepared to share the opportunity and three guests who get involved because they can visualize themselves doing the business. One person can be the trainer for the entire city, so you never project the idea that a person would have to get up in front of a group to be successful.

It is very important to get your distributors together at least once a week. Remember Napkin Presentation #8 on Sizzle Sessions? You need to keep your "logs" together to promote the proper energy so your distributors will be more effective when talking to their friends.

It is not necessary to spend a lot of money for meeting facilities. There are many restaurants that have a back or side room you could use at no extra charge. Simply talk to the manager and explain to him that you have a group of people you would like to get together with on a weekly basis. You start your meetings by 8:00 p.m. and you will be gone by 9:30. You will invite your people to come early (6:30 to 7:00) to have dinner before the meeting. He won't need to put on extra help since the orders can go in as they each arrive. Also if the server gets busy, you are not concerned about speedy service. The restaurant manager and/or owner will be happy with this arrangement and so will the server. Finally, be sure to encourage your people to tip well.

This arrangement should not cost you anything above your meals and tips. The distributors who do not wish to eat should come about 7:45.

We have found with this type of social setting it is very comfortable for your distributors to have a guest. You may even want to offer to buy your guest's dinner or coffee. (This makes your meals or coffees a deductible business expense.) Once he has signed up, he is on his own.

It is okay to invite your guest to your training meeting even if he has not yet seen your twenty-minute presentation. He will see it as the instructor is teaching the distributors how to present it. When making your invitation, emphasize that he is coming to a training session and not to an opportunity meeting. He will see the opportunity during the training.

71

Notes

Chapter XV

Important Phrases and Handling Objections

As I pointed out in Napkin Presentation #4, your business should look like a large building under construction. You can't see the building until it begins to rise, and it can't begin to rise until you have laid a solid foundation. In network marketing, you can't see your income (anything substantial) until you have laid your foundation there as well.

Talking to a non-sales type: "I can see you have doubts about getting involved. I want you to understand that if you say yes, I will be training you. Also understand that if I didn't think you could do it, we would be talking about something else."

The question you should ask of yourself about the above is, "Why would I want to talk someone into getting involved in my business if I didn't think he could do it?" You may want to also mention, "Once you have been in the business thirty days and know just a fraction about the business that I do, you will understand why I am so excited about your opportunity."

"Do I have to sell?" No. The products will move in the process of building your business, sharing them with your friends. Have you ever seen a presentation of crystal, siding, cookware, fire alarms, or vacuum cleaners? This is what most people think selling is. The definition of selling comes from 95 percent non-sales types and what they think selling is all about. They define selling as calling on strangers, trying to talk them into buying something they probably neither need nor want. You never have to do that in network marketing. First, you are dealing with people you know. Second, you should be handling products they need and want.

"Is it a pyramid?" No. The major difference between network marketing and pyramids is that pyramids are illegal. Network marketing has been around for over thirty years, and if network marketing were illegal, it would have been shut down long ago. When you get this objection, in most cases, I believe it is due to a fear of failure. The person you are dealing with is afraid to try your program, and by asking if it is a pyramid, he thinks he will get you off his back because most distributors don't know how to respond.

"I can't afford to go into business." A person can get started in most network marketing companies for under $100. Unless they want to spend the rest of their lives working for someone else, they can't afford not to go into business. My definition of "having it made" is having more money than you can spend and the time to spend it. In my opinion, it is a fact that you will never "have it made" working for somebody else.

"My wife/husband won't be interested." Don't let that hold you back. In most cases, it is only one partner that initially gets a business started. Once it becomes successful, the other spouse will come on board. When this happens, your business can really take off. In network marketing, when a couple builds their business together, it's not 1 + 1 = 2; it's 1 + 1 = more. You get a synergistic effect that is really powerful.

"Is there an advantage in being directly sponsored by a company?" No. As a matter of fact, I would consider this to be a disadvantage. The more distributors you have between you and the company, the better. Everyone in your up-line should be helping and supporting your activities. When you are sponsored by the company, you are on your own.

"How far down-group should I work?" The further, the better. Many distributors will not work beyond their pay level. I think this is a mistake. Remember Napkin Presentation #9? When you work beyond your direct pay levels, you are putting heat under the distributors that you are getting paid on.

"How do I select a network marketing company?" By the time you read this, you will probably already be with a company. The truth is, most people don't pick their first company. Somebody they know who is already with a company picked them.

"Can I work with more than one program?" To answer this properly, I need to divide companies into two categories: major-effort programs, those programs that have breakaways and some minimum requirements, and the mail-order and uni-level types. Most people cannot handle more than one major-effort program. You could have several of the latter on your list as long as you understand that the activity with these programs should support your major-effort program. There's an old saying that if you have lots of irons in the fire and one of them is hot, you don't need the rest. Most distributors who are in one major-effort program will gravitate toward spending their time with the one that works best for them.

"I just don't have the time." There are four elements to recruiting and sponsoring: 1) contacts, 2) time, 3) energy, and 4) knowledge. If I am dealing with a very busy person, I simply say, "I'm not asking for your time, just your contacts. Bring up the idea of network marketing to your friends and have them contact me. In other words, we will use your contacts, my time, my energy, and my knowledge. You might spend two minutes, but I'll spend two hours."

"What is the difference between recruiting and sponsoring?" Recruiting is when you bring someone into your organization who is already experienced in network marketing. Sponsoring has the connotation of bringing someone new into network marketing to whom you are making a commitment to train regarding how the industry operates. You can build quickly by recruiting. However, you can build solidly by sponsoring.

Contest idea: Your people enter the contest by sponsoring someone who has never been in network marketing. The new person signed a statement that this is his first company. You may enter as many times as you wish. As the new person reaches various achievement levels, the trainer would receive awards and prizes.

"My sponsor doesn't help me. What should I do?" Go up-line until you find someone who will. Eventually your sponsor, if inactive, will drop out and you will move up-line under the one who is helping you.

"How important are potlucks?" Anytime you do something positive to bring your distributors together, you are creating energy.

"There is a town about two hours' drive from my home. I know five people there. Should I attempt to sponsor all five myself or should I sponsor one and put the rest under the one?" You should never put anyone under anyone else unless you have brought the two parties together and there will be a mutual benefit and support. I would sponsor the best one first. Then, have some Sizzle Sessions so you can introduce the other four to the first one. If they get along, great. If they don't, you will end up doing the work anyway, so you may just as well sponsor them yourself.

"My company says I can't join another company." It is interesting to note that some companies have this attitude. They are happy to recruit distributors away from other companies, but it's a gross no-no if someone does it to them. These are the same companies that say, "Come with us and earn your freedom." As soon as you do, they are the ones who want to own you.

"I am happy with my company, so why should I join another one?" We believe in supporting our industry, network marketing. When we want something for our family, we would prefer to join a company and buy the product wholesale than buy from a retail or direct sales outlet. You can be signed up with a lot of companies to buy products wholesale; however, few distributors will be successful if they try to build an organization with more than one.

"I am burned out on network marketing. My company just declared Chapter 11." This would be like going to town, eating out, getting a bad meal, then deciding that every restaurant in town is bad. Remember, you cannot fail in network marketing. You can only quit. If your company goes belly-up, find another one. Never quit. On your tombstone visualize these two possible epitaphs (put your name in the blanks): A.) "Here lies _____, a person who tried once in life and quit," or B.) "Here lies _____, a person who never made it but never quit trying."

"When should I quit my regular job?" Many distributors get the urge to go full-time too soon. This is a major mistake. It puts too much pressure on them to make money NOW. It is difficult to work on your foundation when the rent is due this week. You shouldn't quit your job until you have built up a reserve and you are making at least twice as much from your network marketing efforts as you are making from your regular job. Remember, your bonuses only come once a month (with most programs). Most people are used to getting paid weekly. Some spell it "weakly."

Notes

Notes

Chapter XVI

Why Network Marketing

When you understand the following presentation, you will see why 90 percent of the population should be in network marketing.

In most countries, the name of the game is to work until you retire and accumulate enough funds so you can live comfortably until you die. Living on social security would not be considered living comfortably. When you are living in the home of your choice (with no mortgage payment) and driving the car of your choice (with no car payment); when your credit cards are all paid up and you have no phone bill—in other words, you have no bills—when you are in this situation and have $10,000 coming to you each and every month whether you get out of bed or not, you would have a lifestyle better than most millionaires.

For most people to have $10,000 coming in every month, it would take $2,400,000 in the bank at 5 percent interest. Refer to Chart #1 and you will see how much money it takes at various interest rates to produce various monthly incomes. Pick the income you would like to have, then see how much you would have to accumulate to be able to get it. Remember, before you can accumulate, you have to make the money, pay your taxes, mortgage, car payment, and all of your bills. How much do you really have left to accumulate?

So we now know it takes:

$2,400,000 to give you $10,000 per month.

Cut this in half:

$1,200,000 to give you $5,000 per month.

How many people do you know who could accumulate $1,200,000 to $2,400,000 by the time they retire?

A person in network marketing can in two to five years build a part-time income of $5,000 to $10,000 per month. This money will spend the same as the money he would get from 5 percent interest on $1,200,000 to $2,400,000.

The above example is where you could be in two to five years with your residual income. Let's take a look at the first few months to one year.

It takes $48,000 in the bank to produce a $200 monthly income. How many people do you know who could save $48,000 in three months? Almost anyone, using our system, could build an organization that would pay them $200 per month.

Note the following:

$48,000 in the bank to produce $200 monthly income

$24,000 in the bank to produce $100 monthly income

$12,000 in the bank to produce $50 monthly income

$6,000 in the bank to produce $25 monthly income

$3,000 in the bank to produce $12.50 monthly income

How many people do you know who could save $3,000 to $6,000 per month? Most people would say no one. How many people do you know who could sponsor one friend a month? Remember, this only takes forty-five seconds of talking, then loan them the book to read the first four Napkin Presentations. Then get them together with your sponsor. This can be done with a three-way call. Isn't it interesting that anyone using this system can sponsor one friend a month and teach him to do the same.

Note: If you only sponsored one a month and taught your people to do the same, your organization would look like this:

1	Month	2
2		4
3		8
4	Month	16
5		32
6		64
7		128
8		256
9		512
10		1024
11		2048
12		4096

What if you only did this once a year and taught your people to do the same? You would be financially independent by the end of twelve years. How many people would love to be retired in twelve years? One a month would get you there in one year!

Network marketing is not a numbers game like sales. A salesperson goes to work for a sales manager. Network marketing is the opposite. When you sponsor someone, you get to go to work for them. You get to choose whom you go to work for!

What you really need to do to be successful in network marketing can be said in two sentences:

1. Make a friend (if you don't have one).

2. Meet his friends.

""ARE YOU SECURE IN YOUR RETIREMENT?""

Do you know how much money you require in the bank to receive the amount of money you would like to have at retirement? To "OWN YOUR OWN LIFE" means to us, that you would be able to do the things that you would like to do and not worry about the cost!!!! The following chart shows the percentage of interest being paid by the financial institutions and the amount of money you would be required to have to generate the monthly amount that would meet your needs. Find the amount you would like to have and then the current interest rate being paid by the financial institutes and see how much you need to save to retirement!

$200.00 per month.		$600.00 per month.		$800.00 per month.		$1000.00 per month.	
INT. RATE	AMOUNT IN THE BANK	INT. RATE	AMOUNT IN THE BANK	INT. RATE	AMOUNT IN THE BANK	INT. RATE	AMOUNT IN THE BANK
2%	$ 120,000.00	2%	$ 362,000.00	2%	$ 480,000.00	2%	$ 600,000.00
3	80,000.00	3	240,000.00	3	320,000.00	3	400,000.00
4	60,000.00	4	180,000.00	4	240,000.00	4	300,000.00
5	48,000.00	5	144,000.00	5	192,000.00	5	240,000.00
6	40,000.00	6	120,000.00	6	160,000.00	6	200,000.00
7	34,286.00	7	102,857.00	7	137,143.00	7	171,429.00
8	30,000.00	8	90,000.00	8	120,000.00	8	150,000.00
9	26,666.80	9	80,001.00	9	106,667.00	9	133,334.00
10	24,000.00	10	72,000.00	10	96,000.00	10	120,000.00

$2000.00 per month.		$4000.00 per month.		$5000.00 per month.		$10,000.00 per month.	
INT. RATE	AMOUNT IN THE BANK	INT. RATE	AMOUNT IN THE BANK	INT. RATE	AMOUNT IN THE BANK	INT. RATE	AMOUNT IN THE BANK
2%	$ 1,200,000.00	2%	$ 2,400,000.00	2%	$3,000,000.00	2%	$6,000,000.00
3	800,000.00	3	1,600,000.00	3	2,000,000.00	3	4,000,000.00
4	600,000.00	4	1,200,000.00	4	1,500,000.00	4	3,000,000.00
5	480,000.00	5	960,000.00	5	1,200,000.00	5	2,400,000.00
6	400,000.00	6	800,000.00	6	1,000,000.00	6	2,000,000.00
7	342,857.00	7	685,714.00	7	857,143.00	7	1,714,285.00
8	300,000.00	8	600,000.00	8	750,000.00	8	1,500,000.00
9	266,667.00	9	533,334.00	9	666,668.00	9	1,333,335.00
10	240,000.00	10	480,000.00	10	600,000.00	10	1,200,000.00

We have a system whereby you can, by going back to school a few hours per a week to learn how to do it, meaning getting involved, you can secure your financial security at whatever level you wish to work for. We know if you'll learn our system you could be financialy independent in 1-3 years at better than $50,000.00 per a year. How many college graduates go into debt for their education to get a good job, yet are not able to be financialy independent in 1-3 years after graduation at $50,000.00 per a year? I personnally don't know any job except a home based business that can give you this opportunity. If you would like to take advantage of OWNING YOUR OWN LIFE contact the person that gave you this chart

AN INDEPENDANT DISTRIBUTOR:

About the Author

Don Failla started his network marketing career in 1967. He developed a proven system for building a large organization by paying attention to what worked as he built his business.

Today, Don and his wife, Nancy, travel worldwide teaching their proven system as international networking trainers. They live in San Diego and can be reached through www.donandnancyfailla.com. They have two sons, Doug and Greg, and five grandchildren, Christian, Jessica, Joshua, Julia, and Joel.

This book has sold millions of copies and is in many languages. It is a major part of Don's proven system.

Printed in the United States
58425LVS00003B/322-384

9 781600 080098